Frog Fun

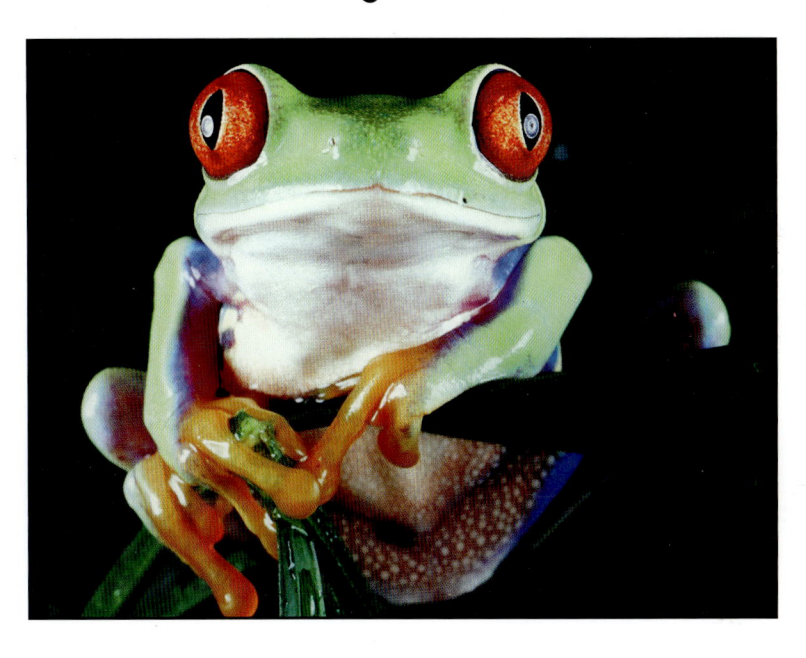

by Kris Bonnell

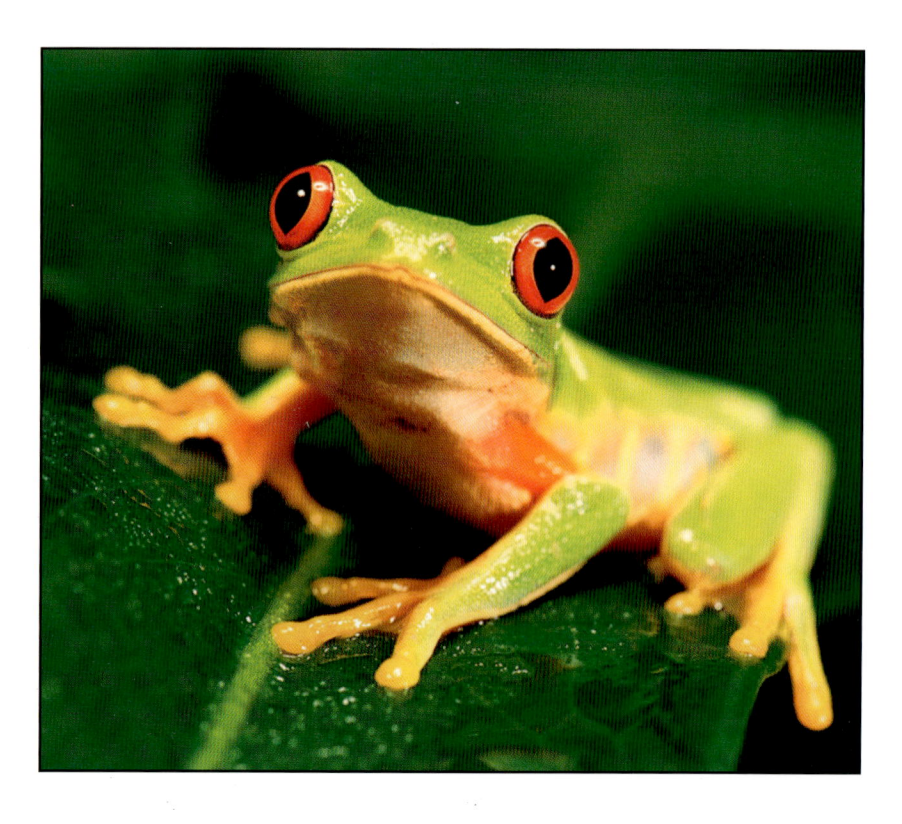

This frog is on a leaf.

Frog Fun

by Kris Bonnell

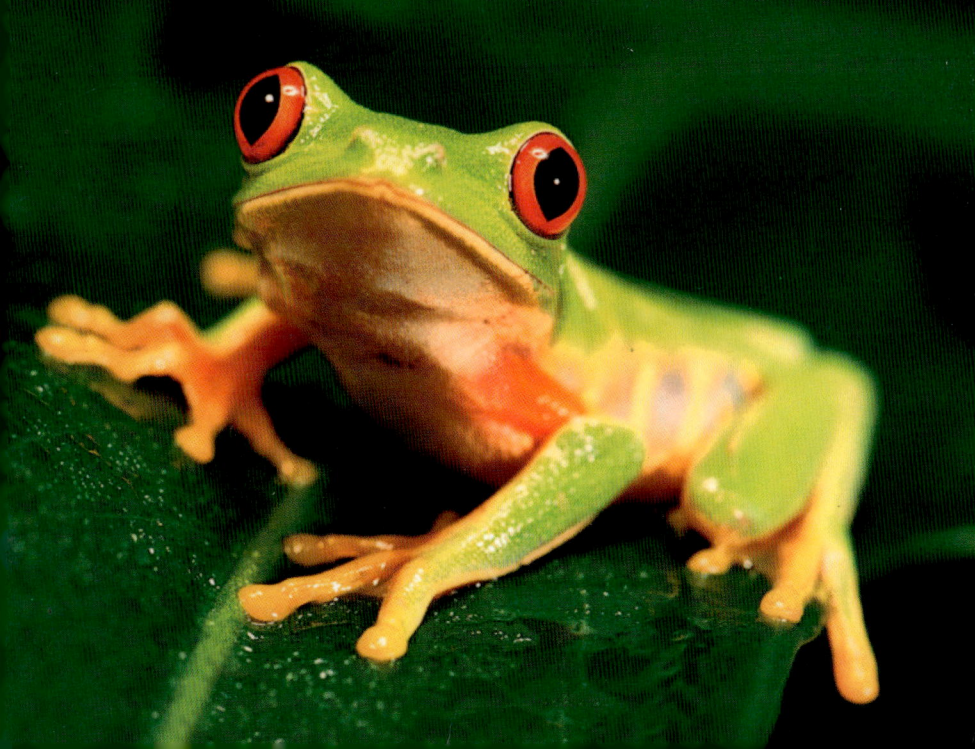

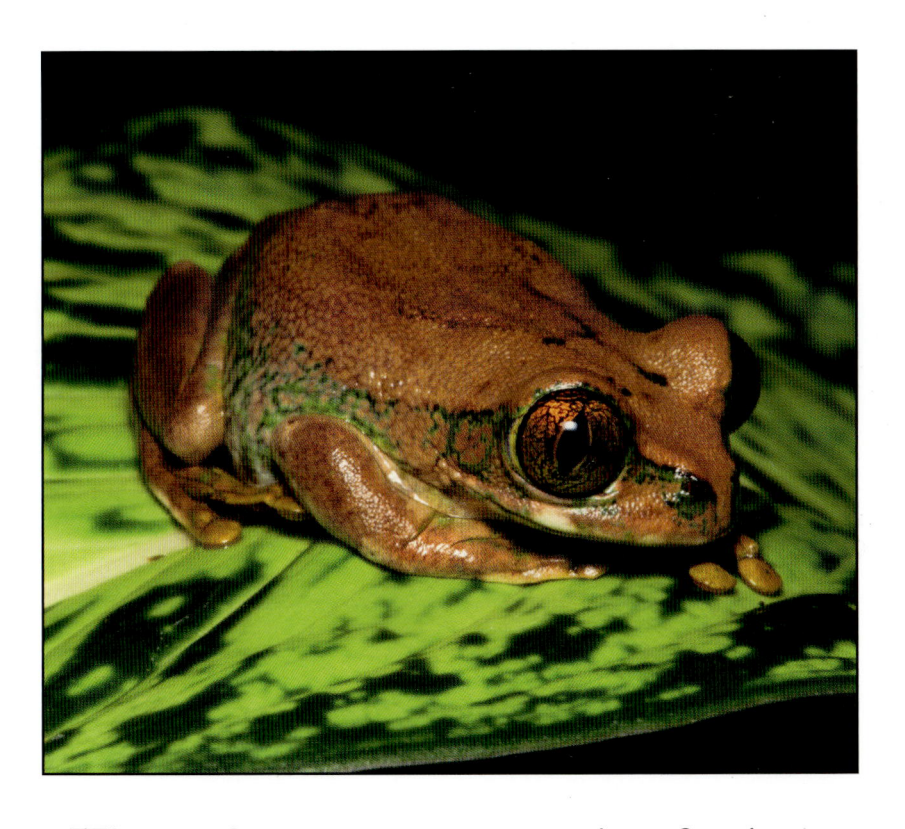

This frog is on a leaf, too.

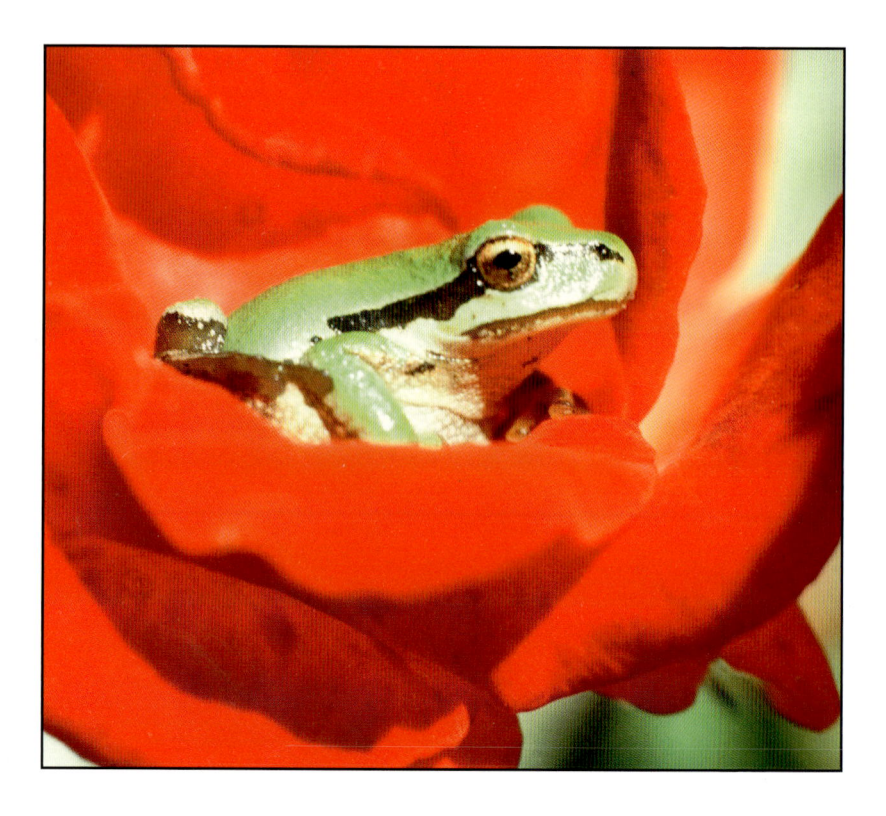

This frog is in a flower.

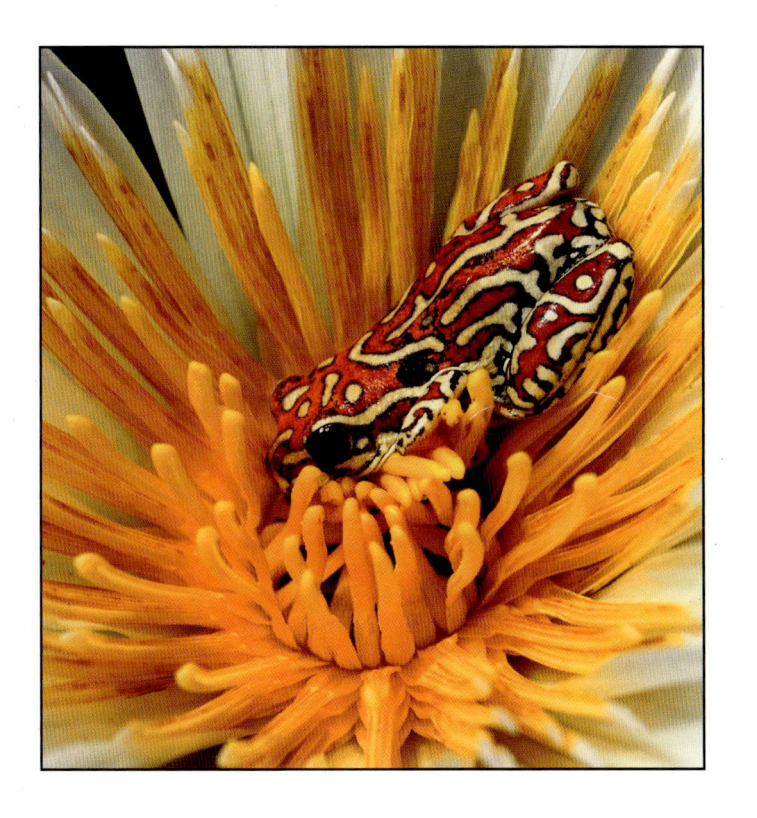

This frog is in a flower, too.

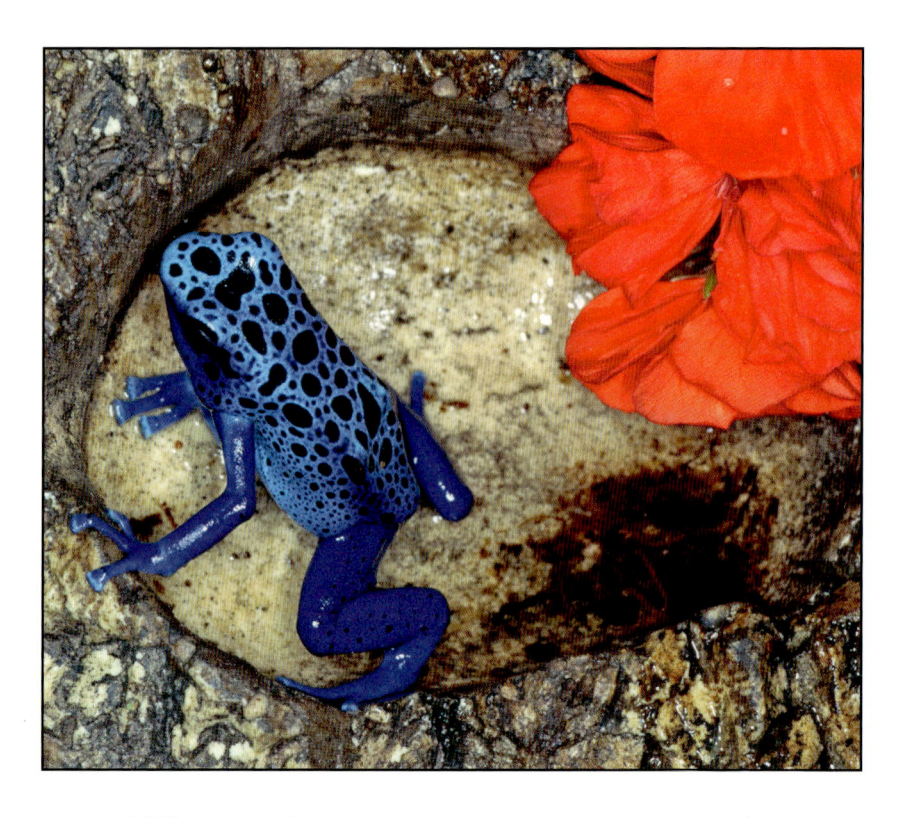

This frog is on a rock.

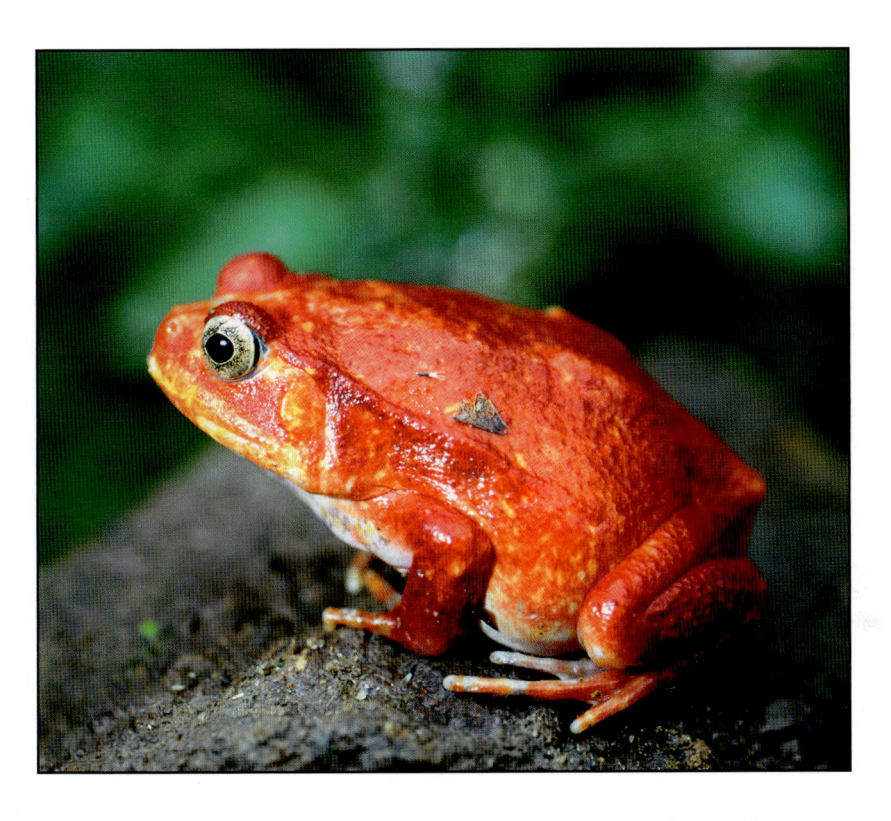

This frog is on a rock, too.

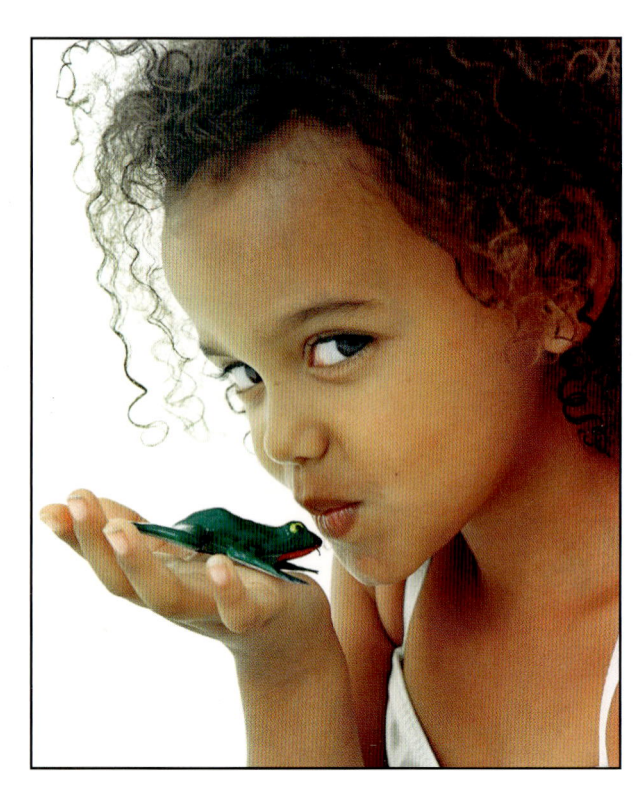

This frog is in my hand!